ADULTPIANO
Adventures

Popular

Arranged by Nancy and Randall Faber

1

Production Coordinator: Jon Ophoff
Editor: Isabel Otero Bowen
Cover: Terpstra Design, San Francisco
Engraving: Dovetree Productions, Inc.

FABER
PIANO ADVENTURES

ISBN 978-1-61677-188-1

OREWORD

Popular songs connect a generation. And special songs take us back to special moments. This book enables you to reconnect to those melodies and those times at the piano. You'll find songs by the Beatles, Adele, Elton John, Ed Sheeran, Richard Marx, and Louis Armstrong, along with hits from movies and musicals.

Adult Piano Adventures® Popular Book 1 is designed for adult beginners and for those who have played piano in the past and are reacquainting with the keyboard. Those exploring the piano for the first time will find the arrangements appealing and well within reach. Adults returning to the keyboard can "brush up on basics" while exploring timeless hits and popular favorites.

This book has three sections.

- Section 1 features piano arrangements with minimal hand position changes. Many selections include an optional duet part.

- Section 2 introduces the I, IV, and V7 chords in the key of C major. With these three chords, a pianist can play many melodies.

- Section 3 presents the I, IV, and V7 chords in the key of G major.

Enjoy these popular tunes from across the decades.

TABLE OF CONTENTS

My Heart Will Go On

Love Theme from *Titanic*

Music by James Horner
Lyric by Will Jennings

Wistfully

Ev - 'ry night in my dreams I see you, I feel____ you.
Far a - cross the dis - tance and spac - es be - tween____ us,

That is how I know you go on.
you have come to show you go on.

Near, far, wher - ev - er you are I be -

Teacher Duet: (Student plays 1 octave higher)

R.H.

L.H. *pp* *with pedal*

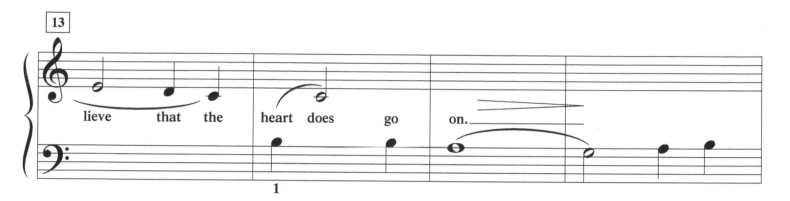

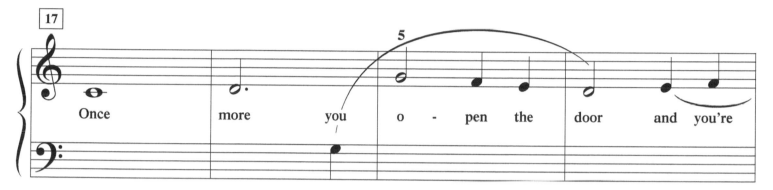

Edelweiss
from *The Sound of Music*

Lyrics by Oscar Hammerstein II
Music by Richard Rodgers

Teacher Duet: (Student plays 1 octave higher)

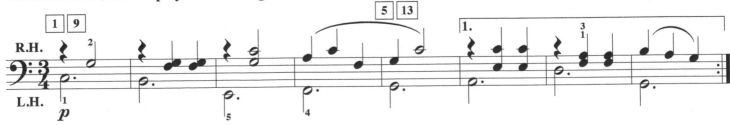

Blos - som of snow, may you bloom and grow,

mf

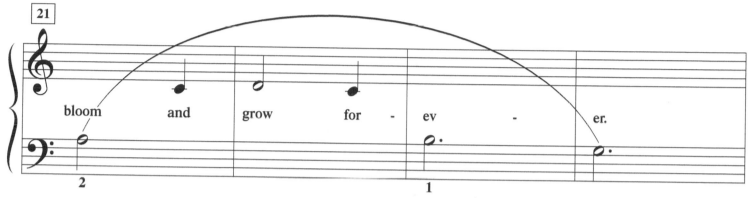

bloom and grow for - ev - er.

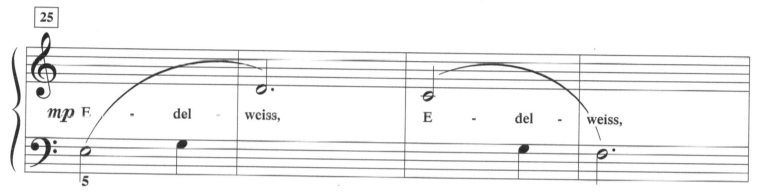

mp E - del - weiss, E - del - weiss,

bless my home - land for - ev - er.

Let It Be

Words and Music by
John Lennon and Paul McCartney

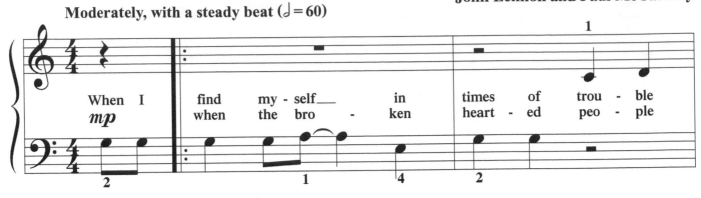

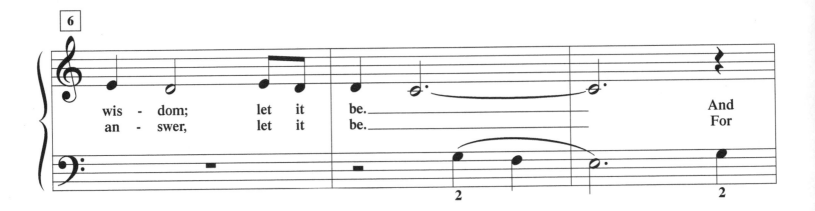

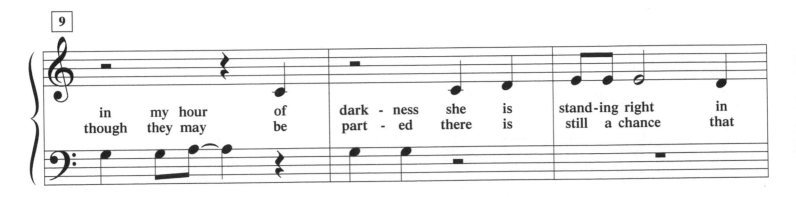

Oh, What a Beautiful Mornin'
from *Oklahoma!*

Lyrics by Oscar Hammerstein II
Music by Richard Rodgers

Teacher Duet: (Student plays 1 octave higher)

Downton Abbey (Theme)

Music by John Lunn

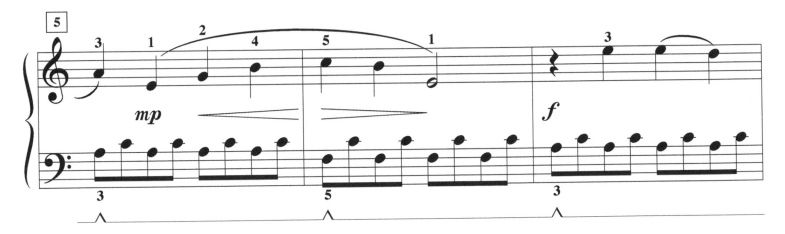

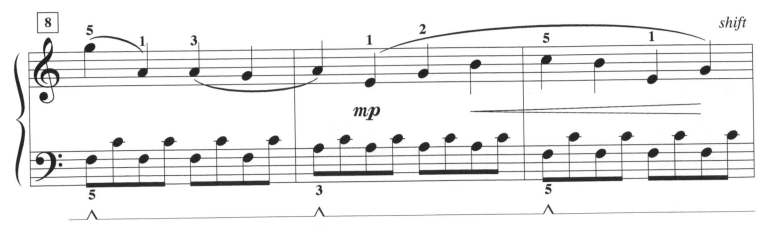

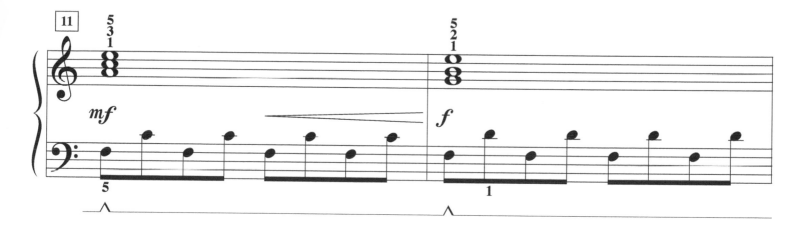

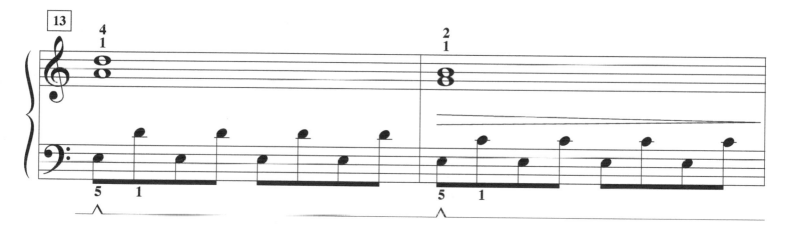

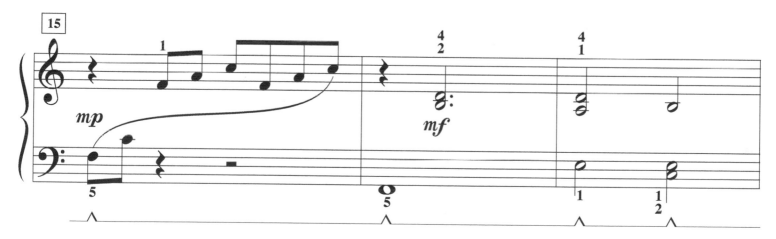

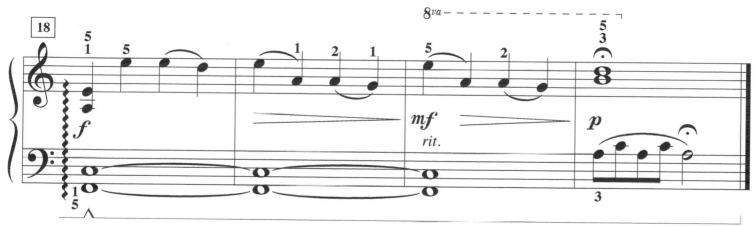

There's No Business Like Show Business

from the stage production *Annie Get Your Gun*

Words and Music by
Irving Berlin

Teacher Duet: (Student plays 1 octave higher)

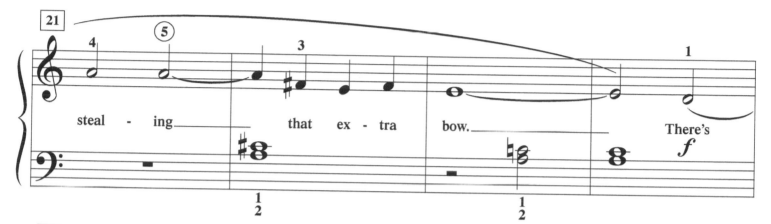

No - where could you get that hap - py feel - ing when you are

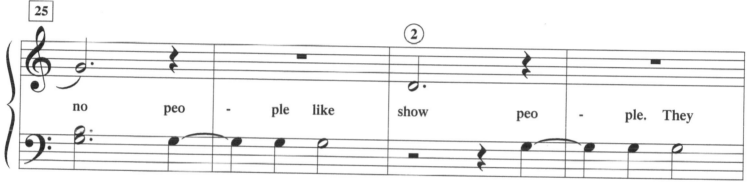

steal - ing_____ that ex - tra bow._____ There's

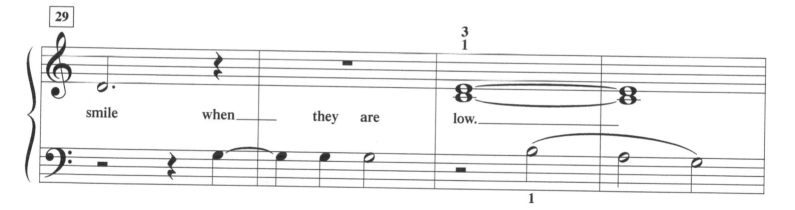

no peo - ple like show peo - ple. They

smile when_____ they are low._____ They

16

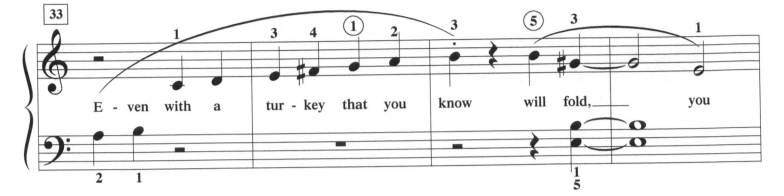

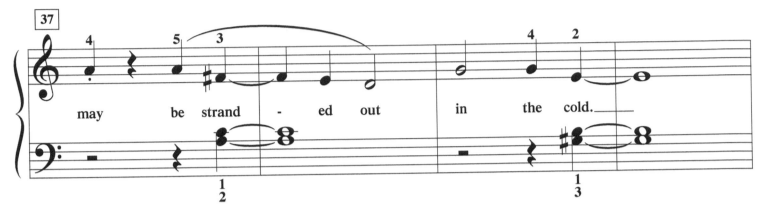

FF3031

Do-Re-Mi
from *The Sound of Music*

Lyrics by Oscar Hammerstein II
Music by Richard Rodgers

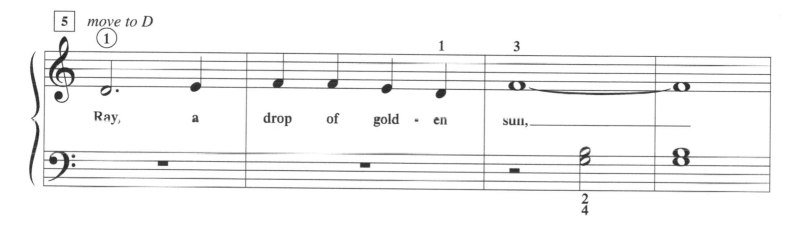

Teacher Duet: (Student plays 1 octave higher)

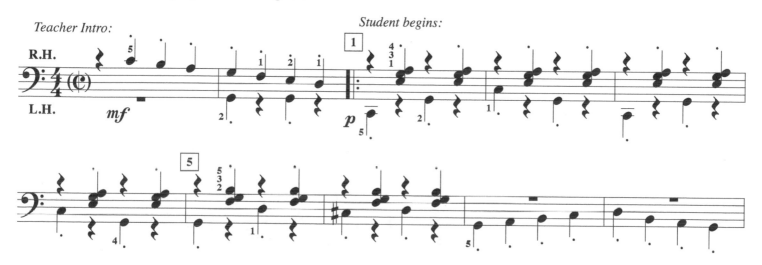

FF3031

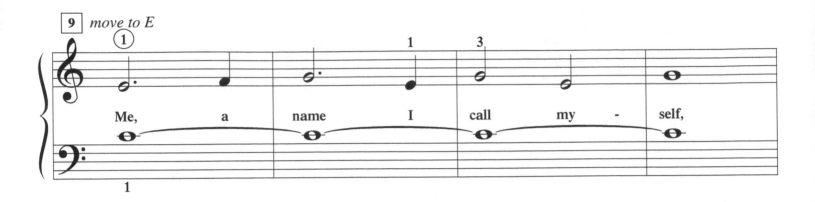

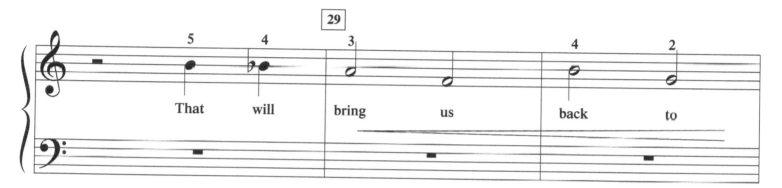

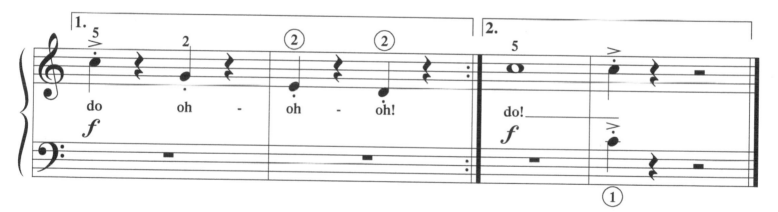

Chim Chim Cher-ee

from Walt Disney's *Mary Poppins*

Words and Music by
Richard M. Sherman
and Robert B. Sherman

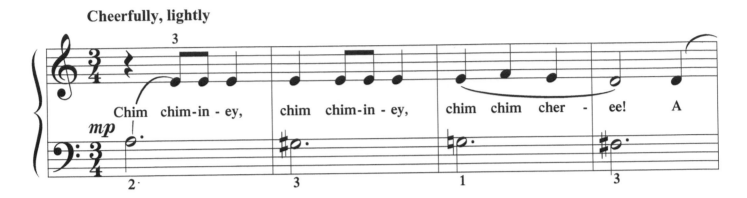

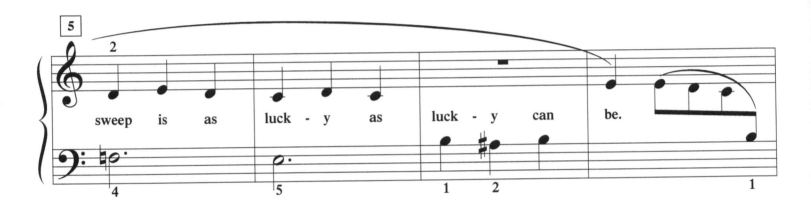

Teacher Duet: (Student plays 1 octave higher)

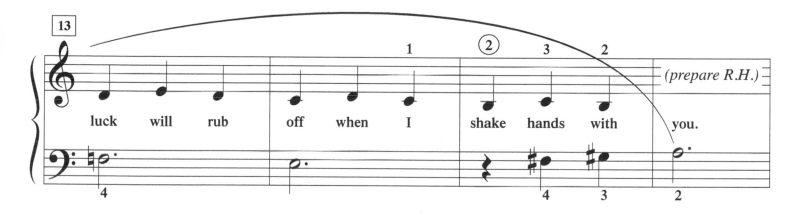

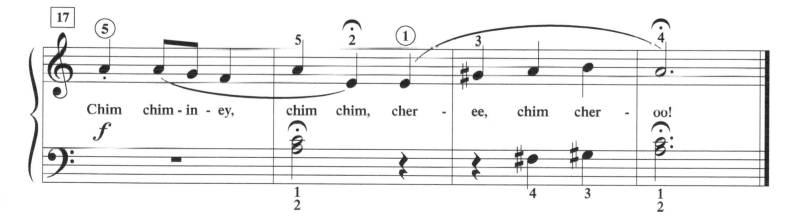

Let's Go Fly a Kite

from Walt Disney's *Mary Poppins*

Words and Music by
Richard M. Sherman and
Robert B. Sherman

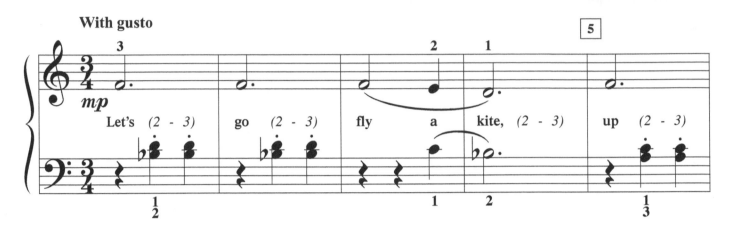

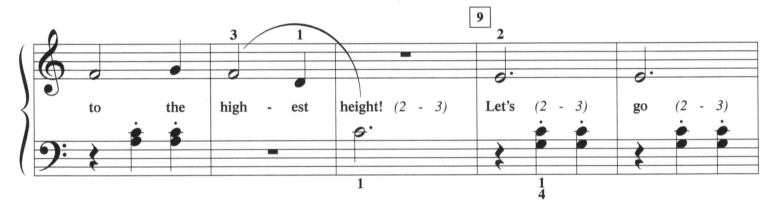

Teacher Duet: (Student plays 1 octave higher)

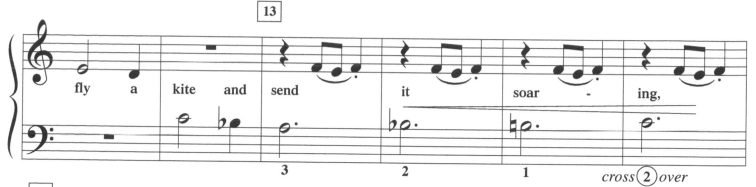

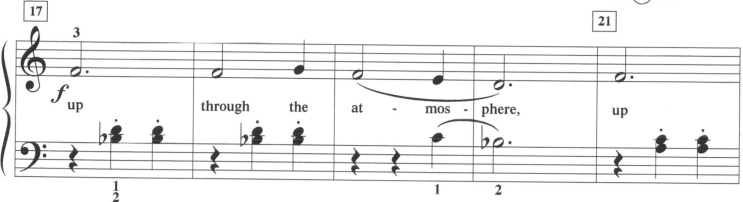

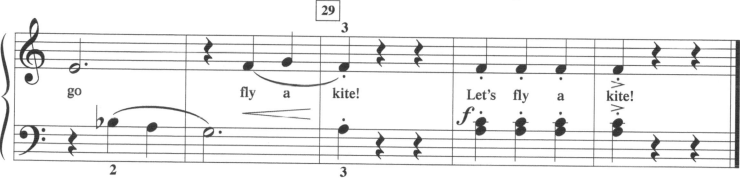

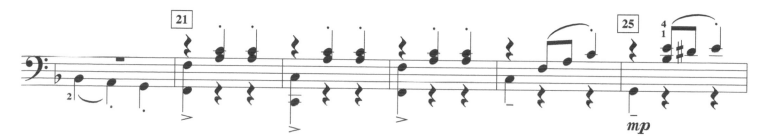

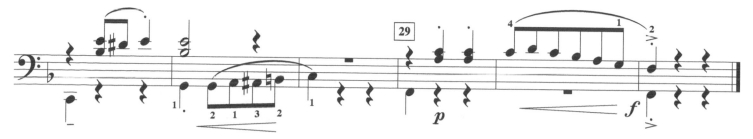

Tomorrow
from the Musical Production *Annie*

Lyric by Martin Charnin
Music by Charles Strouse

Teacher Duet: (Student plays 1 octave higher)

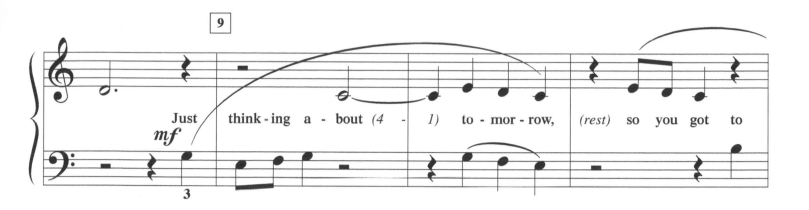

9

Just think-ing a-bout (4 - 1) to-mor-row, (rest) so you got to

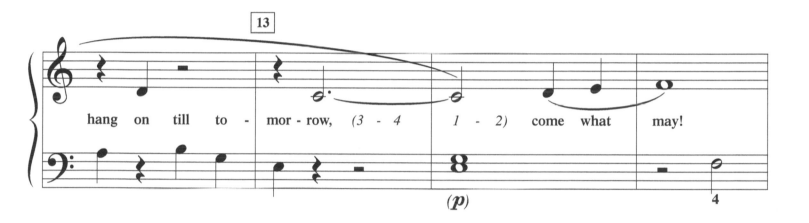

13

hang on till to-mor-row, (3 - 4 1 - 2) come what may!

(p)

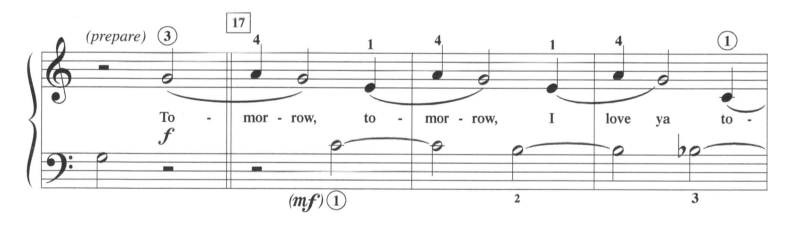

17

(prepare) ③

To-mor-row, to-mor-row, I love ya to-

(mf) ①

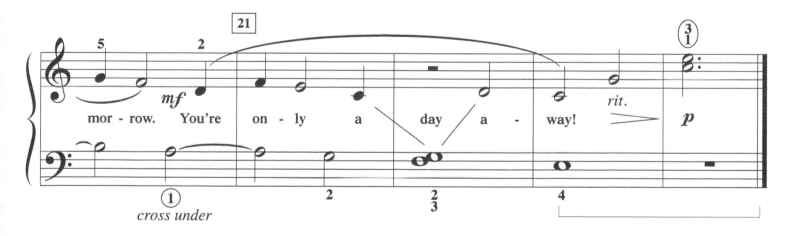

21

mor-row. You're on-ly a day a-way!

rit.

p

cross under

If I Were a Rich Man
from the Musical *Fiddler on the Roof*

Words by Sheldon Harnick
Music by Jerry Bock

Teacher Duet: (Student plays 1 octave higher)

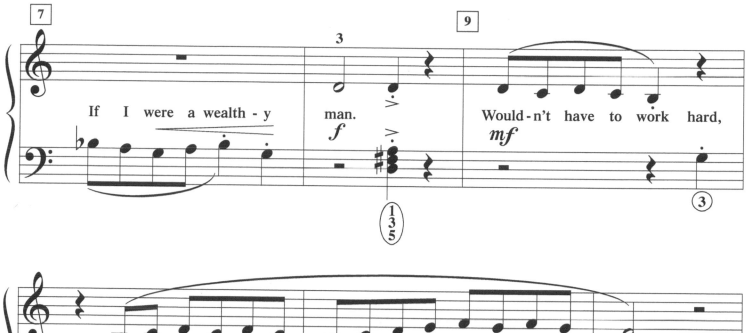

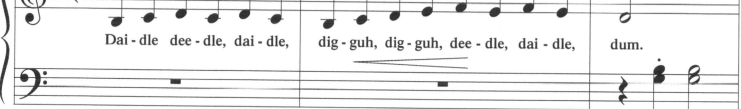

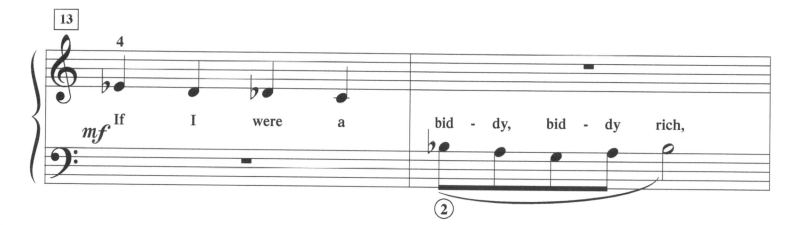

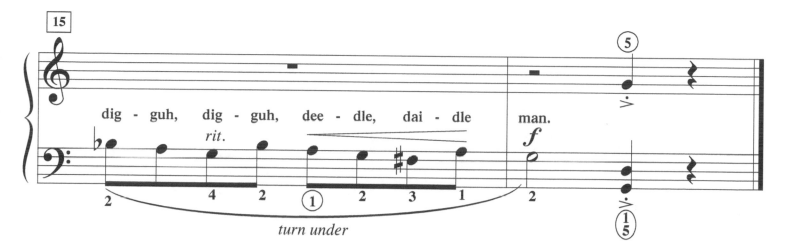

turn under

Climb Ev'ry Mountain

from *The Sound of Music*

Lyrics by Oscar Hammerstein II
Music by Richard Rodgers

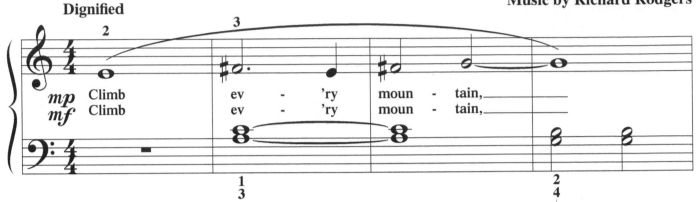

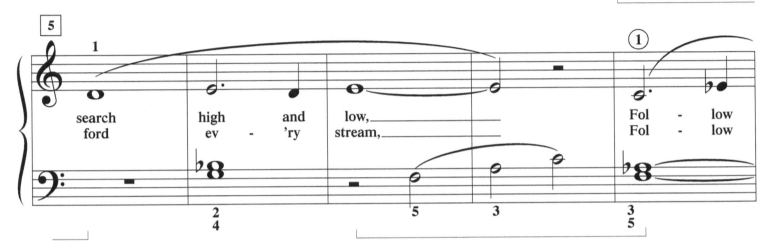

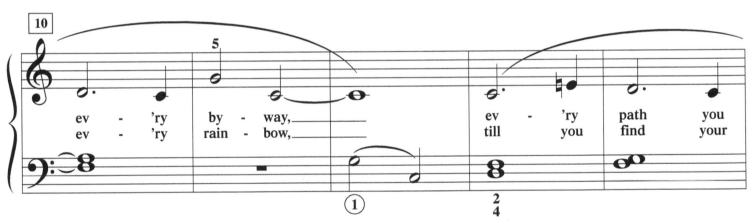

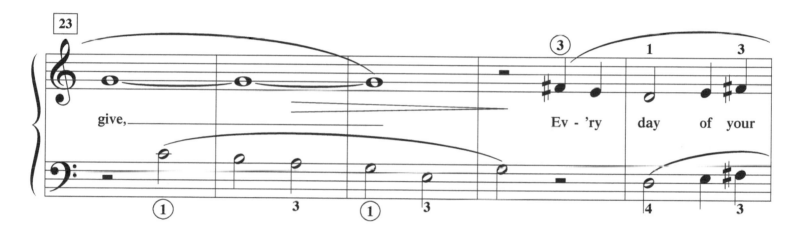

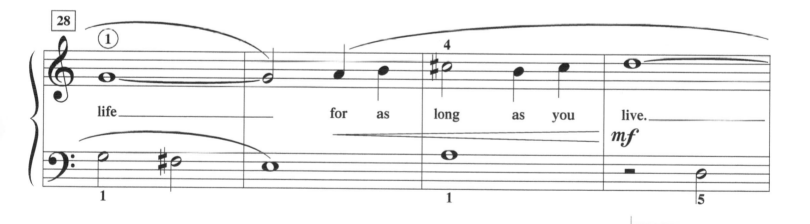

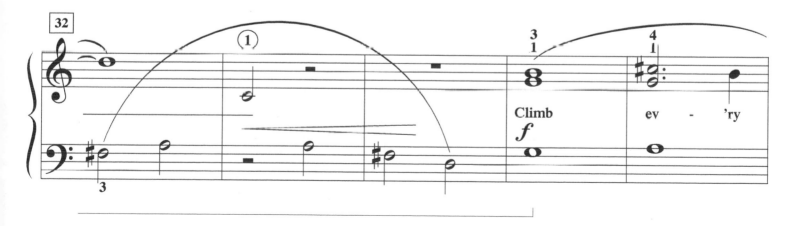

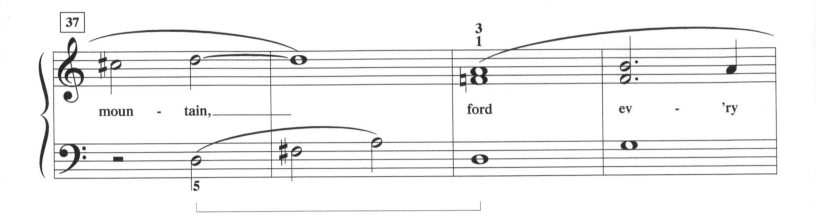

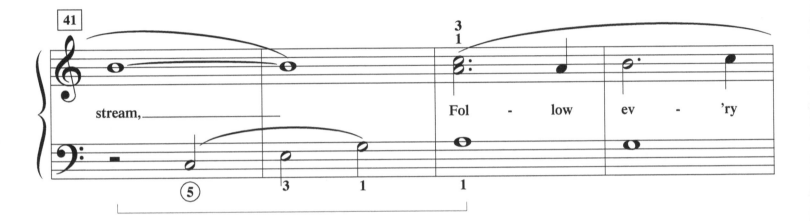

Twist and Shout

Words and Music by
Bert Russell and Phil Medley

Teacher Duet: (Student plays 1 octave higher)

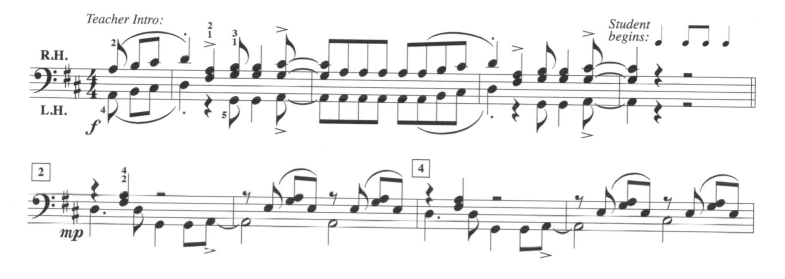

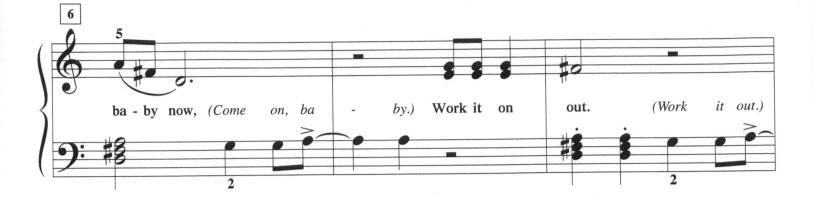

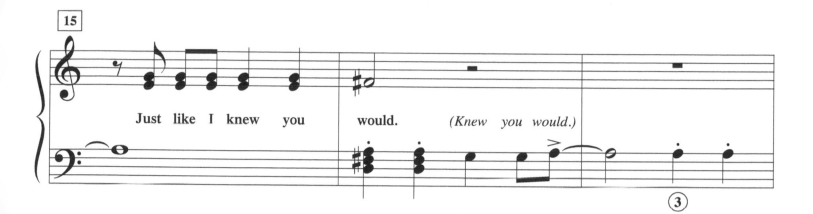

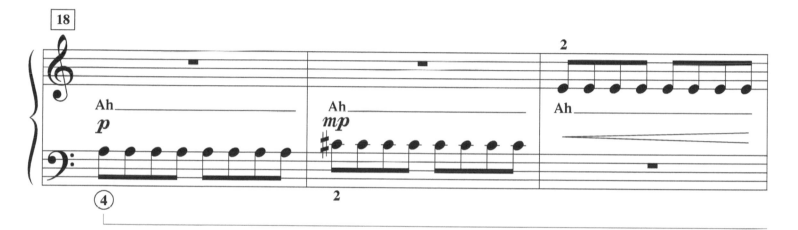

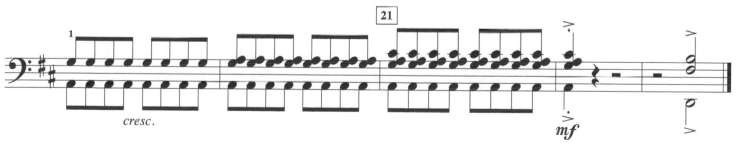

KEY OF C

C Major Scale

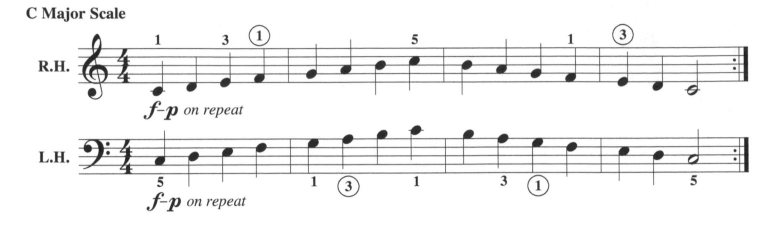

f-p on repeat

f-p on repeat

Primary Chords

The **I**, **IV**, and **V** chords are called the *primary* chords.
They are built on scale degrees 1, 4, and 5 of the major scale.

chord letter names: **C**   **F**   **G**

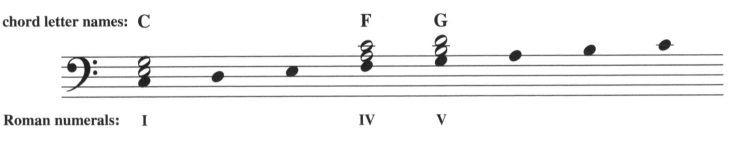

Roman numerals: **I**   **IV**   **V**

C, **F**, and **G** are the **I**, **IV**, and **V** chords in the Key of C.

Common Chord Positions

The chords above are shown in the *root position*, built up in 3rds from the chord *root* (chord name).
By inverting the notes, the **I**, **IV**, and **V7** chords can be played with little motion of the hand.

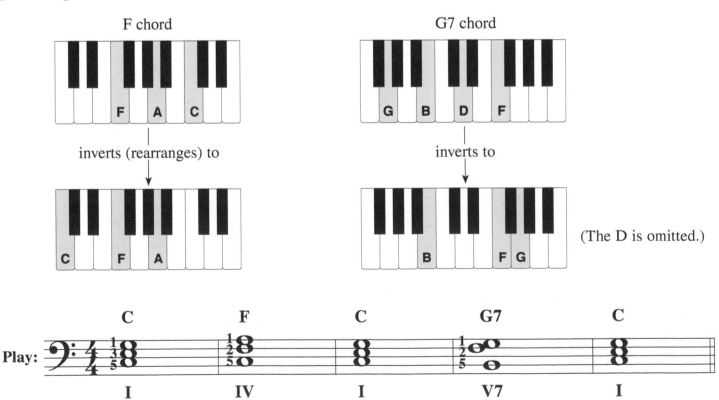

This Land Is Your Land

Words and Music by
Woody Guthrie

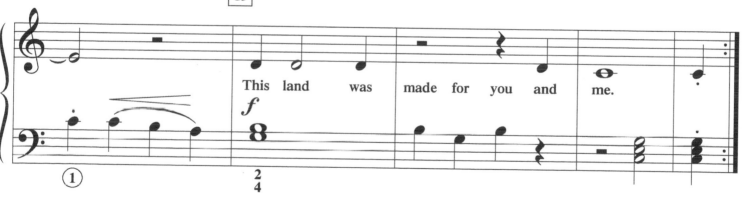

The Tide Is High

Words and Music by
John Holt, Tyrone Evans,
and Howard Barrett

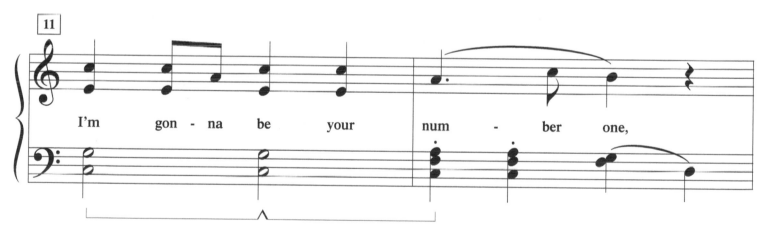

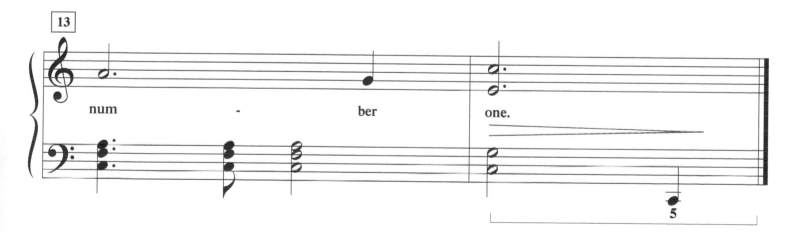

Lean On Me

Words and Music by
Bill Withers

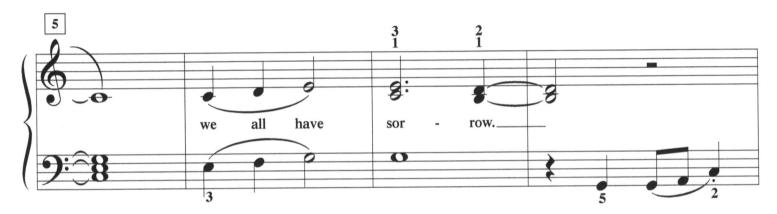

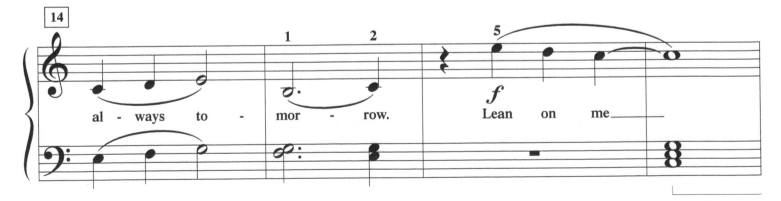

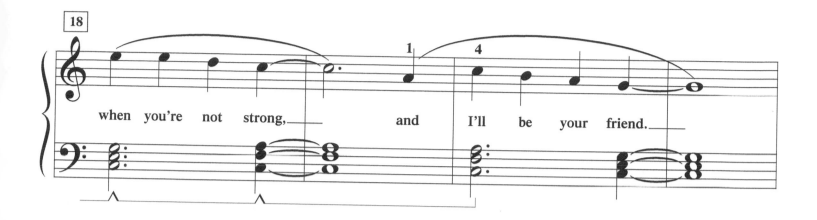

when you're not strong,_____ and I'll be your friend._____

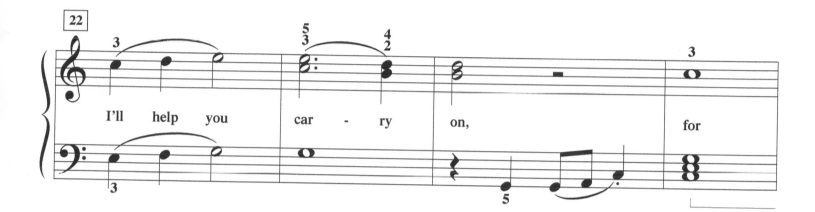

I'll help you car - ry on, for

it won't be long_____ till I'm gon - na need_____ some -

bod - y to lean_____ on._____ *p*

Theme from "Jurassic Park"

from the Universal Motion Picture *Jurassic Park*

Composed by John Williams

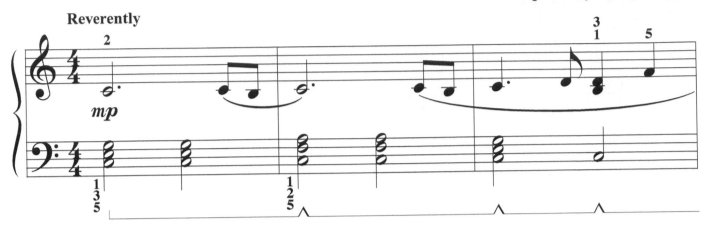

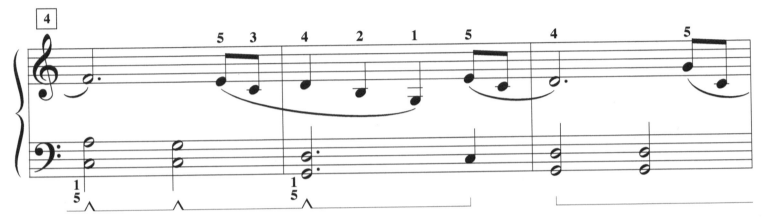

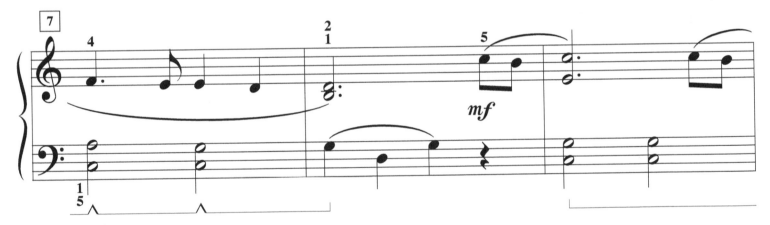

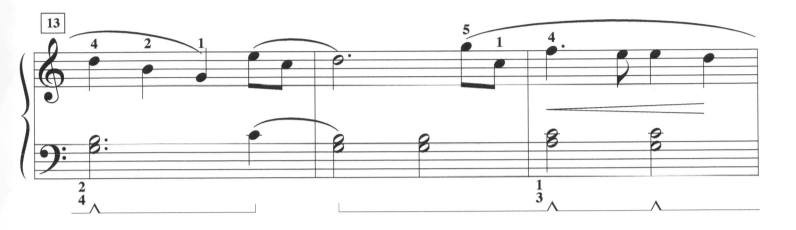

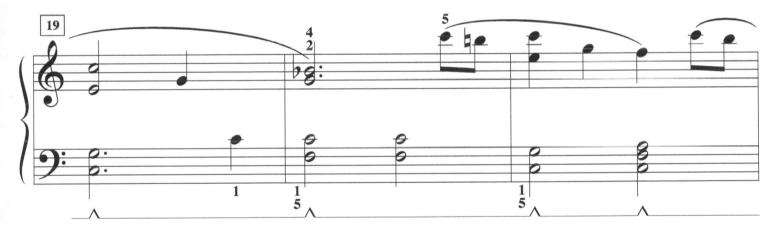

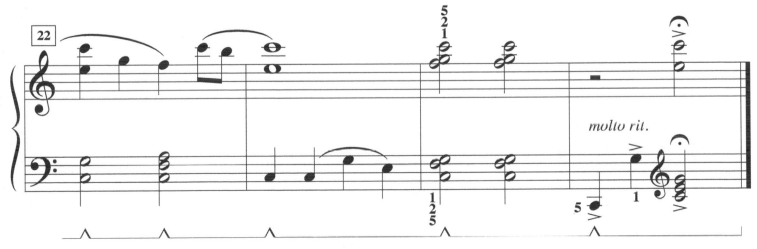

THE VI CHORD

Recall that the **I, IV,** and **V** chords are built on scale degrees 1, 4, and 5 of the major scale.

NEW: The **vi** chord is built on scale degree 6.
Whereas the I, IV, and V chords are major, the vi chord is minor.

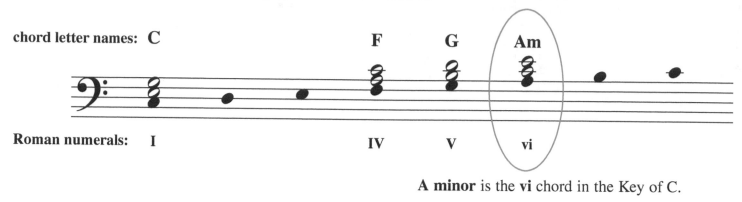

A minor is the **vi** chord in the Key of C.

Common Chord Progressions

Below are two common chord progressions used in popular music.

I–vi–IV–V

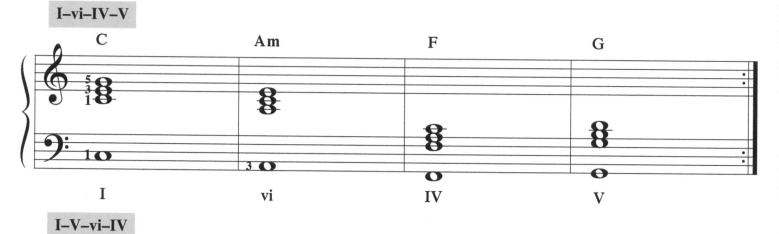

I–V–vi–IV

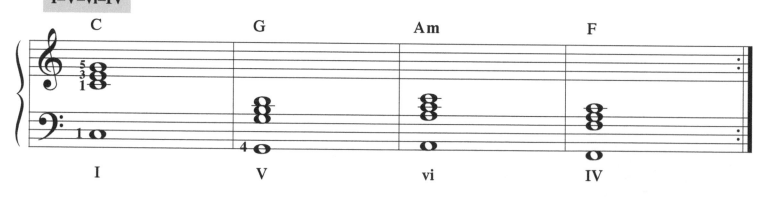

Try these accompaniment patterns for each of the above progressions.

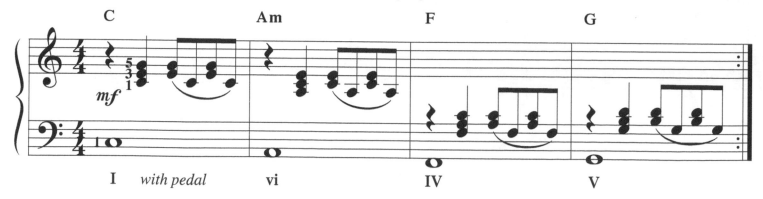

One Call Away

**Words and Music by Charlie Puth, Breyan Isaac, Matt Prime,
Justin Franks, Blake Anthony Carter and Maureen McDonald**

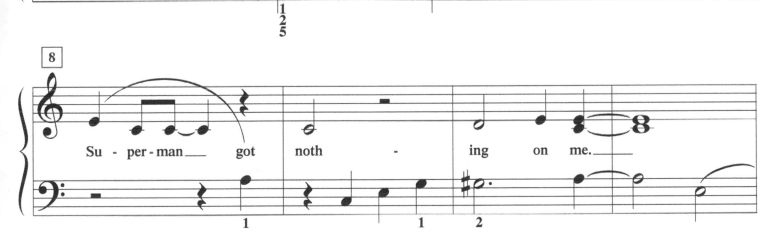

FF3031

Heart and Soul

from the Paramount Short Subject *A Song is Born*

Words by Frank Loesser
Music by Hoagy Carmichael

Moderate swing rhythm

swing the 8ths!

Heart and soul, I fell in love with you.

Heart and soul, the way a fool would do,

cross over

mad - ly, be - cause you held me

tight and stole a kiss in the night.

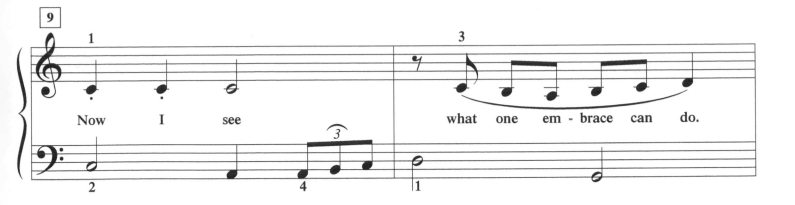

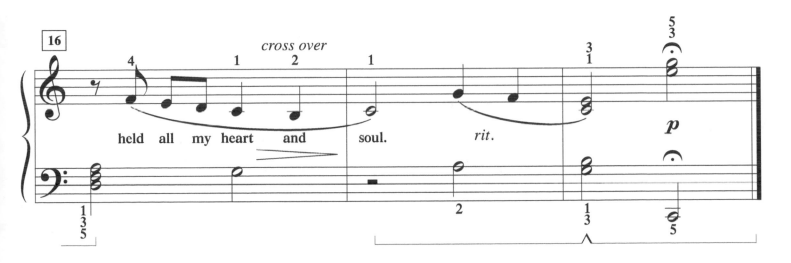

Right Here Waiting

**Words and Music by
Richard Marx**

FF3031

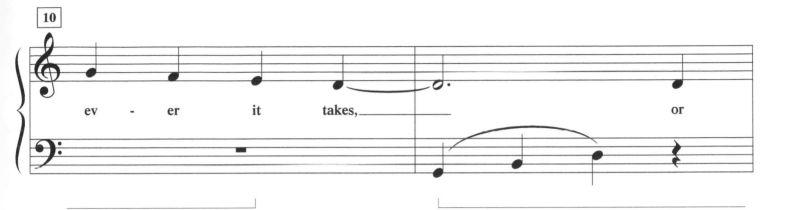

ev - er   it   takes,_____   or

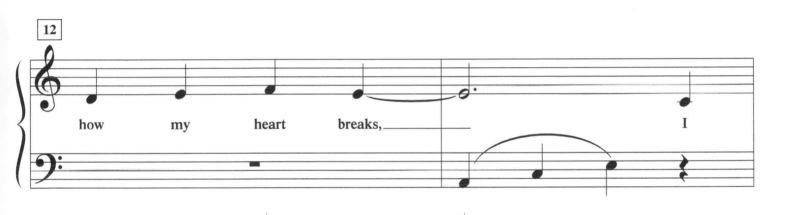

how   my   heart   breaks,_____   I

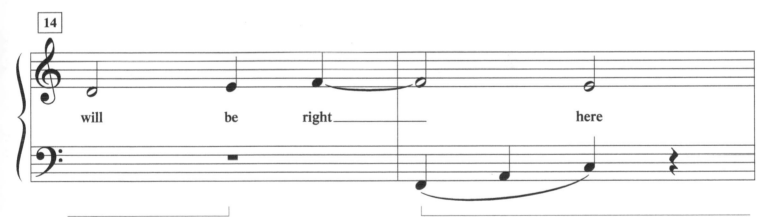

will   be   right_____   here

wait - ing   for   you.   *rit.*

Someone Like You

Words and Music by
Adele Adkins and Dan Wilson

mem - ber   you   said,_____   "Some - times   it   lasts   in love,   but

some - times   it hurts   in -   stead._____   Some - times   it

lasts   in love,___   but   some - times   it hurts   in -

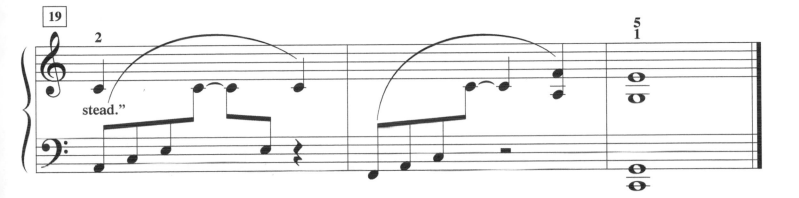

stead."

I Want to Hold Your Hand

Words and Music by
John Lennon and Paul McCartney

Yeah, I'll tell you some-thing I think you'll un-der-

stand. Then I'll say that some-thing,

I want to hold your hand! I want to hold your

hand. I want to hold your hand. Oh,

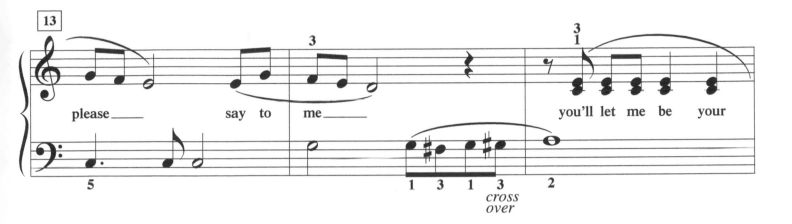

please_____ say to me_____ you'll let me be your

cross
over

man, and please_____ say to me_____

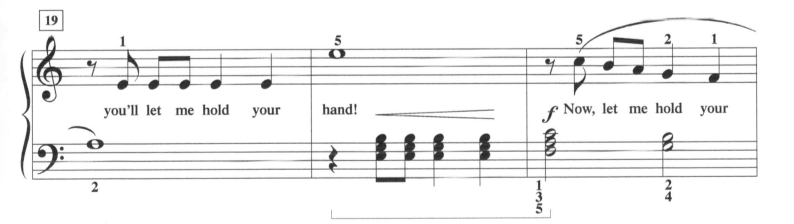

you'll let me hold your hand! *f* Now, let me hold your

hand._____ I want to hold your hand.

Yesterday

Words and Music by
John Lennon and Paul McCartney

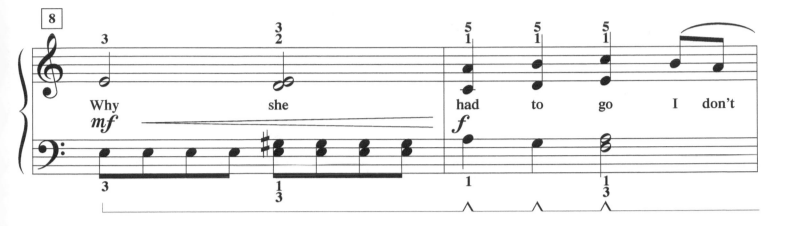

Why she had to go I don't

know, she would-n't say. I said

some-thing wrong, now I long for yes - ter - day.

D.C. al Coda

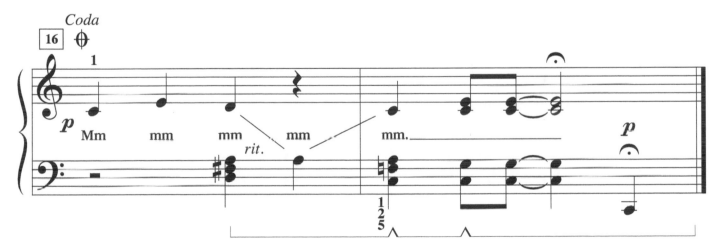

Coda

Mm mm mm mm mm.

The Winner Takes It All

from *Mamma Mia!*

**Words and Music by Benny Andersson
and Björn Ulvaeus**

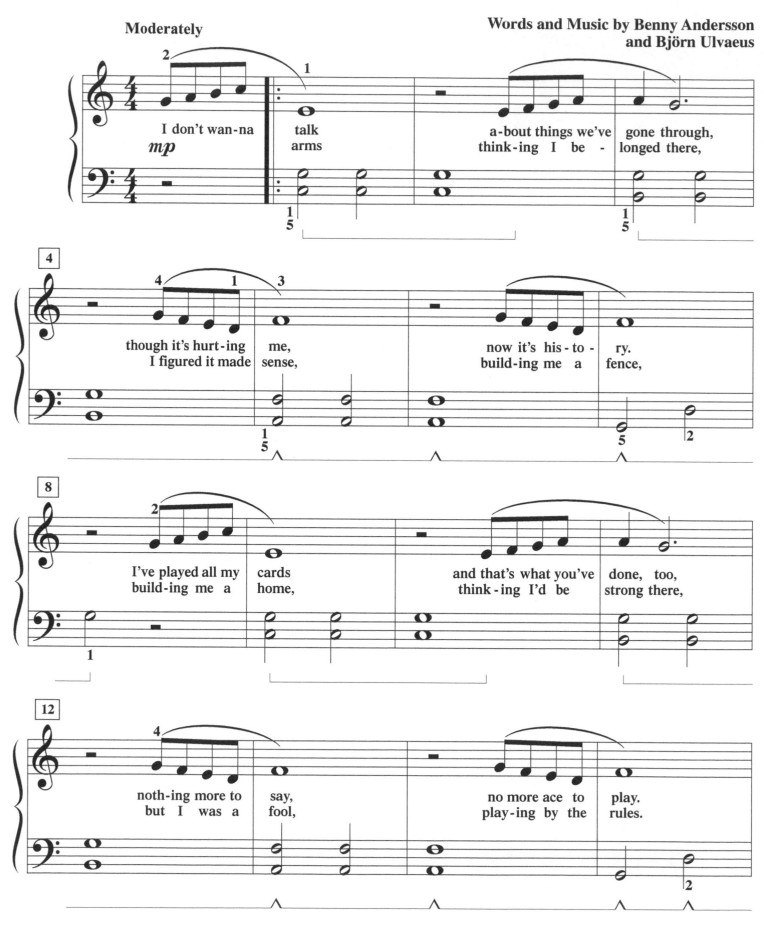

The win-ner takes it all, the los-er stand-ing small
The gods may throw a dice, their minds as cold as ice,

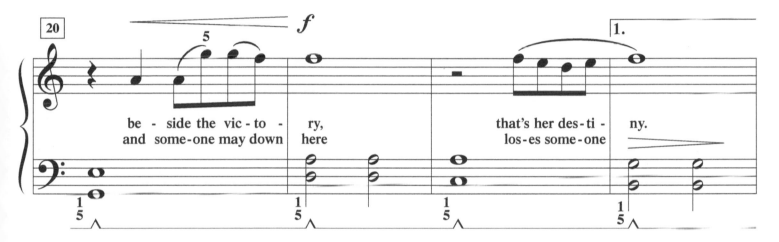

be - side the vic-to - ry, that's her des-ti - ny.
and some-one may down here los-es some-one

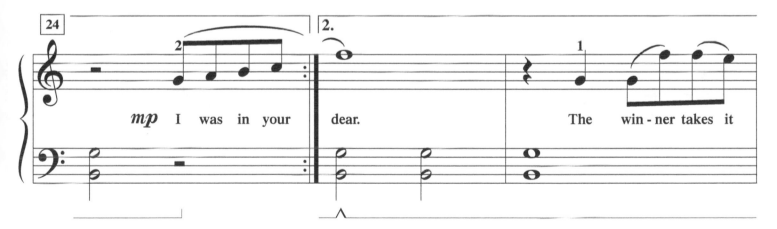

mp I was in your dear. The win-ner takes it

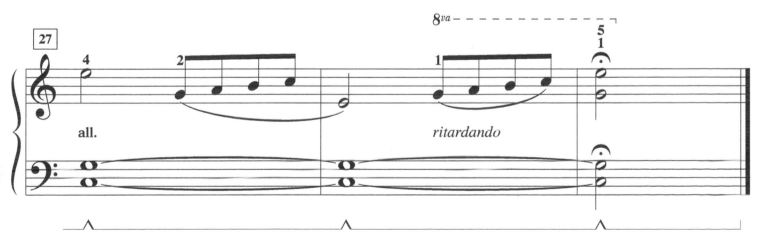

all. *ritardando*

Pachelbel Canon
(Originally in the Key of D)

Johann Pachelbel

Flowing

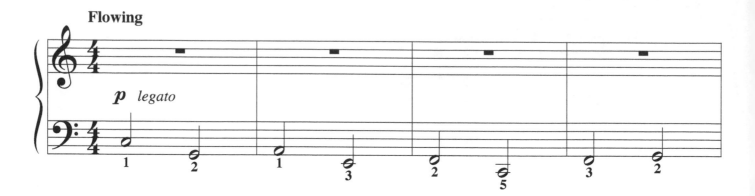

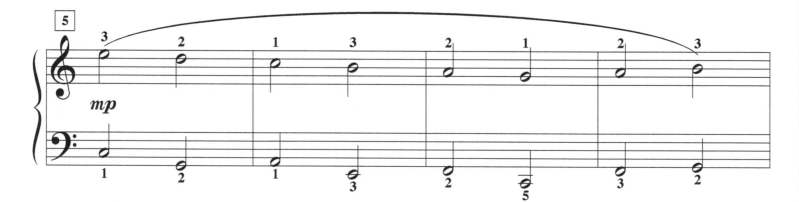

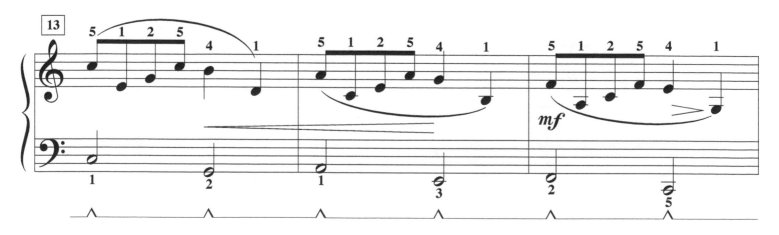

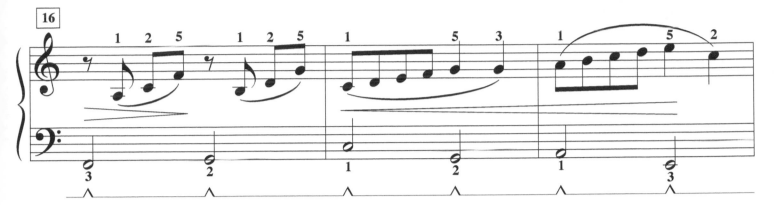

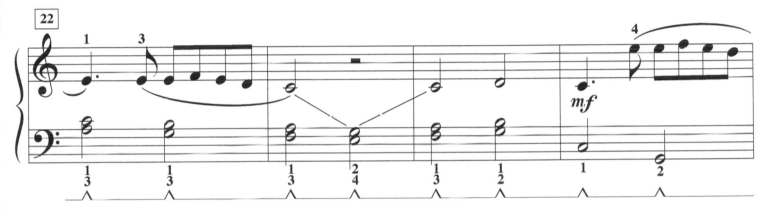

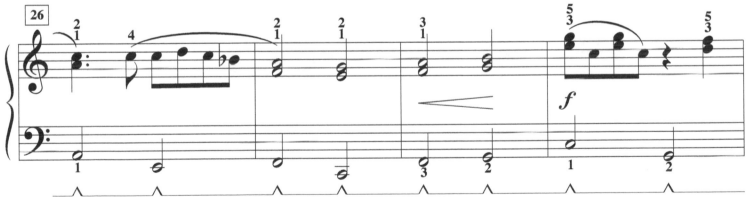

KEY OF G

G Major Scale

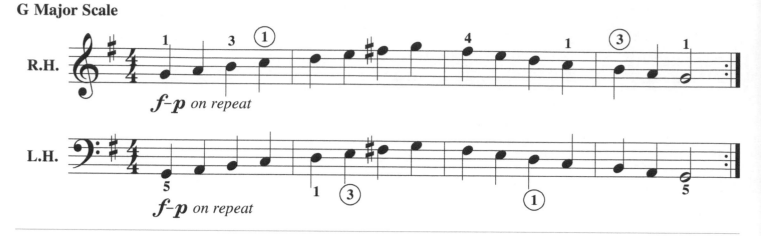

f-p on repeat

f-p on repeat

Primary Chords in G

REVIEW: The primary chords are built on scale degrees 1, 4, and 5 of the major scale.
NEW: Here are the **I**, **IV**, and **V** chords in the Key of G.

chord letter names: **G**   **C**   **D**

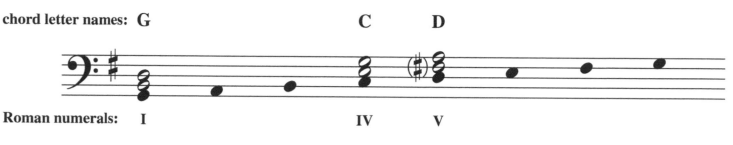

Roman numerals: **I**   **IV**   **V**

In the Key of G the **I**, **IV**, and **V** chords are **G**, **C**, and **D**.

Common Chord Positions

By inverting the notes, the **I**, **IV**, and **V7** chords can be played with little motion of the hand.

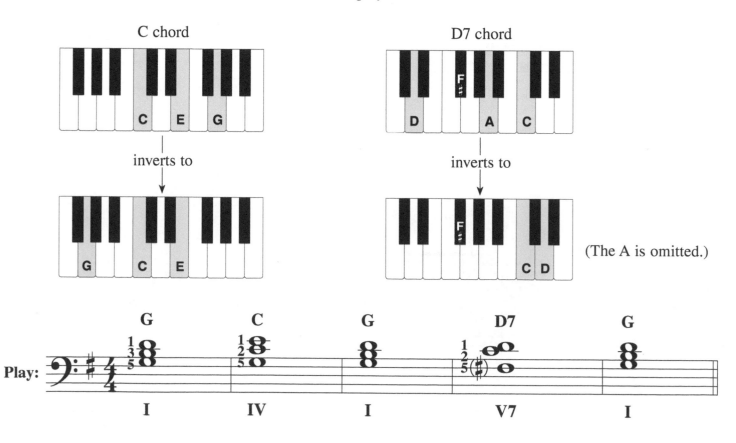

C chord

D7 chord

inverts to

inverts to

(The A is omitted.)

Rocky Top

Words and Music by
Boudleaux Bryant and Felice Bryant

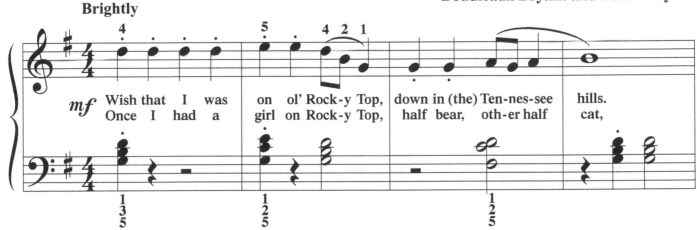

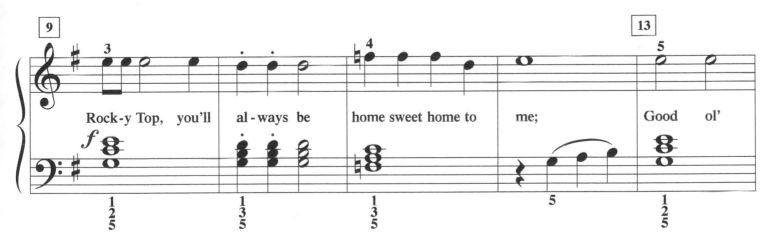

FF3031

Can You Feel the Love Tonight

from Walt Disney Pictures' *The Lion King*

Music by Elton John
Lyrics by Tim Rice

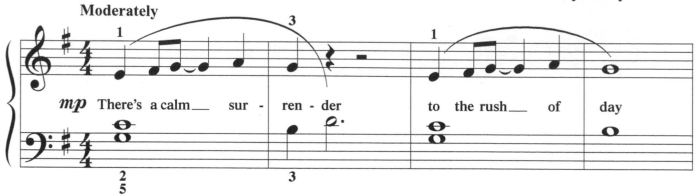

Thinking Out Loud

Words and Music by
Ed Sheeran and Amy Wadge

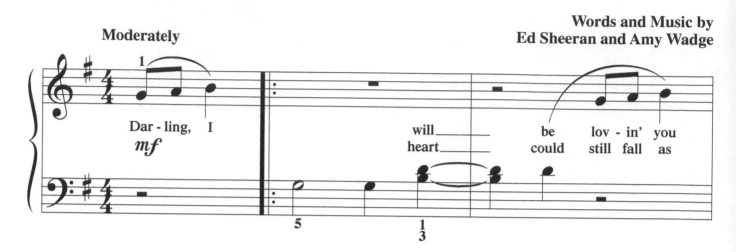

take me in - to your lov - ing arms.

Kiss me un - der the light of a thou - sand stars.____

Place your head on my beat - ing heart.

I'm think - ing out_____ loud,_____ may - be

we found love right where we are.____

Unchained Melody
from the Motion Picture *Unchained*

Lyric by Hy Zaret
Music by Alex North

slow - ly, and time can do so much, Are you still

mf mine? I need your love, I

need your love. God speed your love to

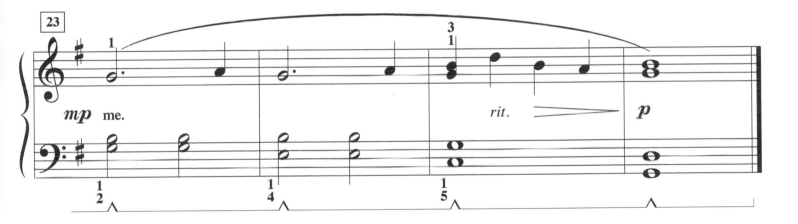

mp me. *rit.* *p*

Angel of Music
from *The Phantom of the Opera*

Music by Andrew Lloyd Webber
Lyrics by Charles Hart
Additional Lyrics by Richard Stilgoe

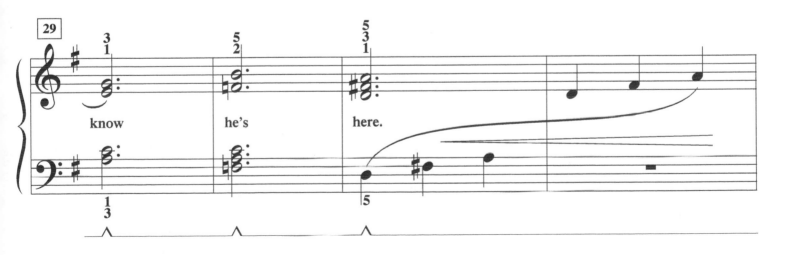

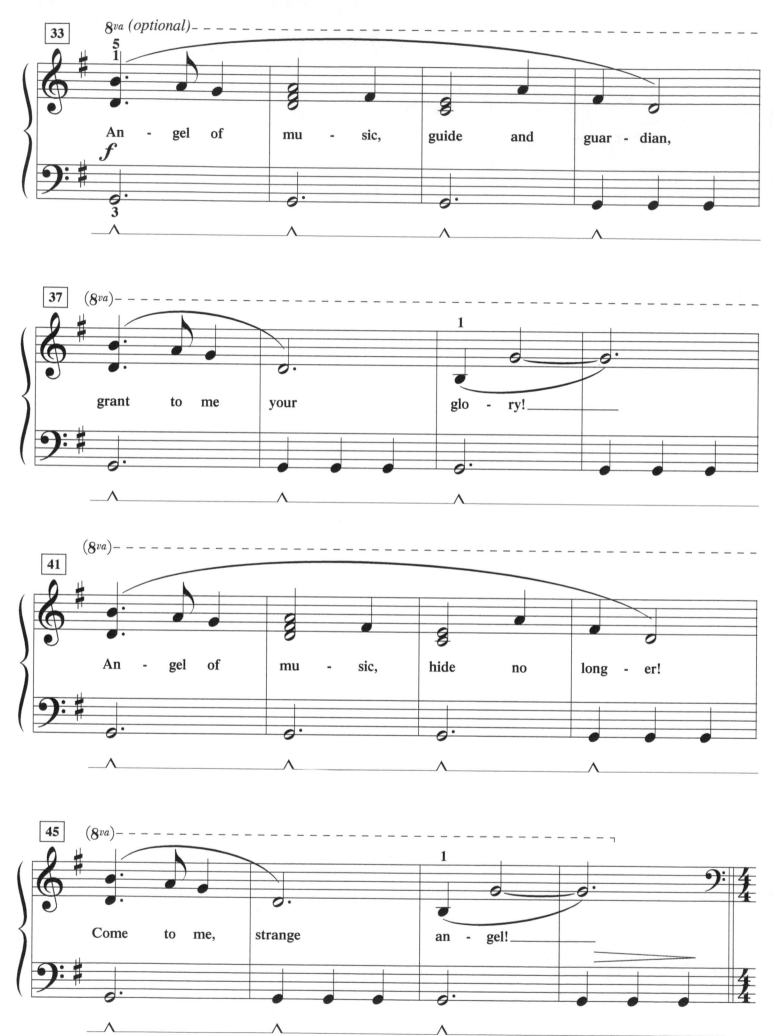

Beauty and the Beast
from Walt Disney's *Beauty and the Beast*

Music by Alan Menken
Lyrics by Howard Ashman

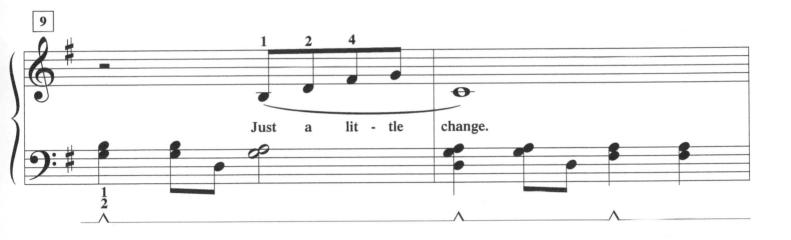

Cer - tain as the sun

ris - ing in the

East.   Tale as old as time,   song as old as

rhyme.   Beau - ty and the   Beast.

Beau - ty and the

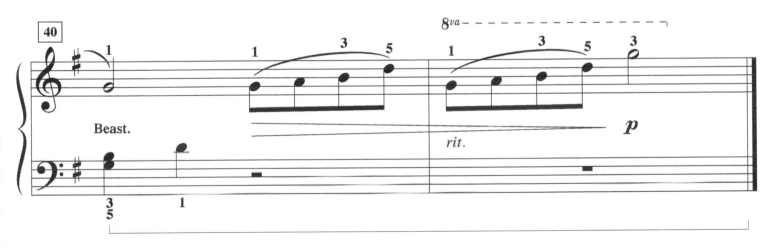

Beast.

Chariots of Fire
from the Feature Film *Chariots of Fire*

By Vangelis

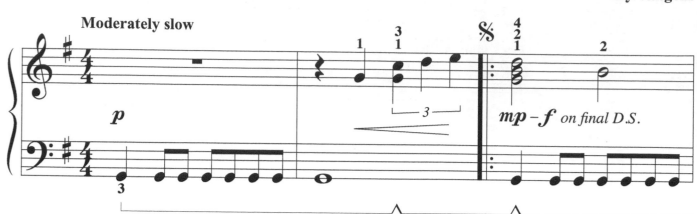

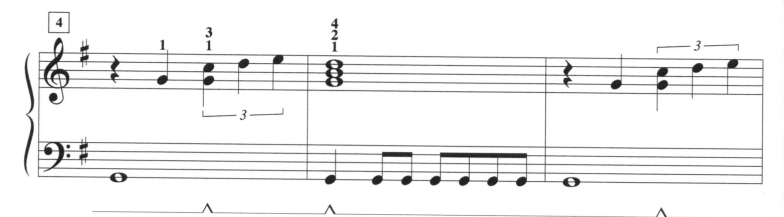

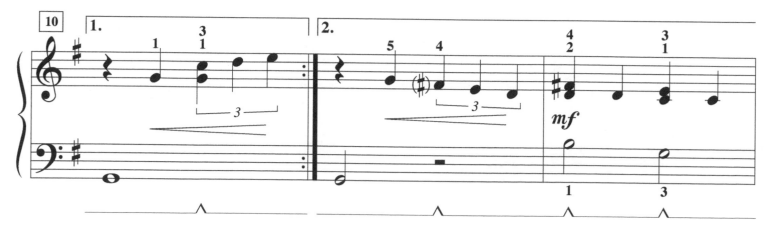

FF3031

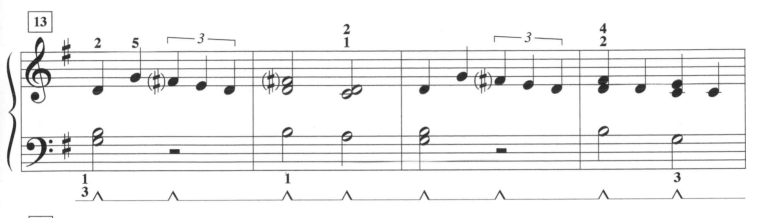

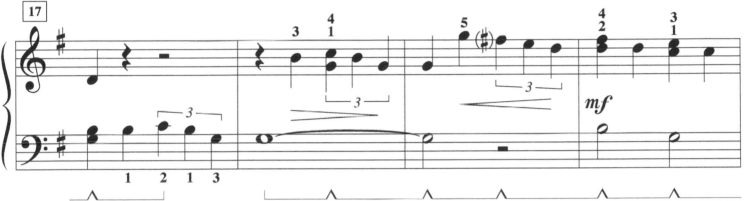

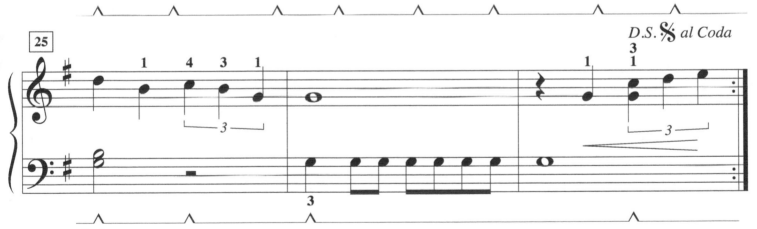

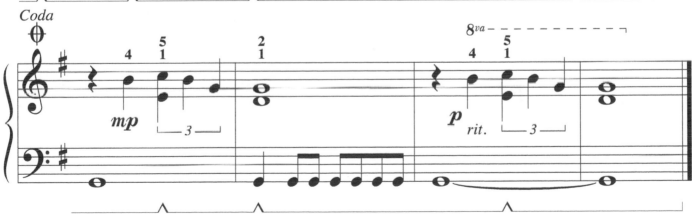

What a Wonderful World

Words and Music by
George David Weiss and Bob Thiele

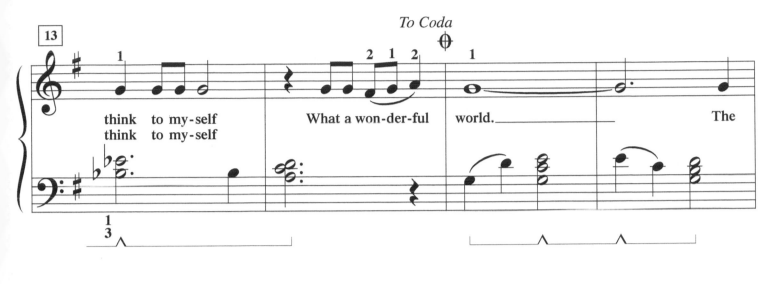

To Coda ⊕

think to my-self What a won-der-ful world._____ The
think to my-self

col-ors of the rain - bow, so pret-ty in the sky, are al - so on the fac - es of

peo-ple go - in' by, I see friends shak-in' hands, say - in', "How do you do?"

D.S. 𝄋 *al Coda*   *Coda* ⊕

They're real-ly say - in' "I love you," I hear

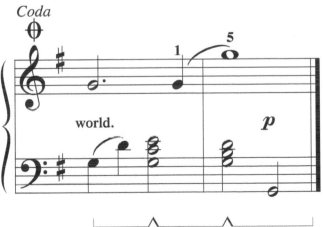

world.   *p*

FF3031

DICTIONARY OF MUSICAL TERMS

DYNAMIC MARKS

pp	***p***	***mp***	***mf***	***f***	***ff***
pianissimo very soft	*piano* soft	*mezzo piano* moderately soft	*mezzo forte* moderately loud	*forte* loud	*fortissimo* very loud

crescendo (cresc.)
Play gradually louder.

diminuendo (dim.) or decrescendo (decresc.)
Play gradually softer.

SIGN	TERM	DEFINITION
	accent mark	Play this note louder.
	accidental	Sharps, flats, or naturals added to a piece and not in the key signature.
	C major chord	A three-note chord built in 3rds above C: C-E-G.
	C major scale	An eight-note scale (C-D-E-F-G-A-B-C) with half steps between scale steps 3-4 and 7-8.
	chord	Three or more tones sounding together.
	I ("one") chord	The Roman numeral I indicates the triad built on scale degree 1.
	IV ("four")	The Roman numeral IV indicates the triad built on scale degree 4.
	V7 ("five-seven")	A four-note chord built up in 3rds from scale degree 5 (often played with only three notes.)
	chord symbol	The letter name of a chord (shown above the staff) indicating the harmony.
	coda	Ending section.
	D7 chord	A four-note chord built up in 3rds from D (D-F♯-A-C). The notes of the D7 chord are often inverted to form a 3-note D7 chord.
D.C. al Fine	**Da Capo al Fine**	Return to the beginning and play until *Fine* (end).
D.S.	**Dal Segno**	Repeat from the 𝄋 sign.
	damper pedal	The right pedal, which sustains the sound, played with the right foot.
	dotted half note	Three counts or beats.
	eighth notes	Two eighth notes equal one quarter note.
	fermata	Hold this note longer than its normal value.
	fifth (5th)	The interval of a 5th spans five letter names. (Ex. C up to G, or A down to D) Line-(skip-a-line)-line, or space-(skip-a-space)-space.
	1st and 2nd endings	Play the 1st ending and repeat from the beginning. Then play the 2nd ending, skipping over the 1st ending.
	flat	A flat lowers a note one half step.
	fourth (4th)	The interval of a 4th spans four letter names. (Ex. C up to F, or G down to D) Line-(skip-a-line)-space, or space-(skip-a-space)-line.
	G major chord	A three-note chord built in 3rds above G: G-B-D. G is the root. B is the 3rd. D is the 5th.
	G major scale	An eight-note scale (G-A-B-C-D-E-F♯-G) with half steps between scale degrees 3-4 and 7-8.
	G7 chord	A four-note chord built up in 3rds from G (G-B-D-F). The notes of the G7 chord are often inverted to form a 3-note G7 chord.

	half note	Two counts or beats (one-half the value of a whole note).
	half rest	Two counts of silence. (Sits on line 3 of the staff)
	half step	The distance from one key to the very closest key on the keyboard. (Ex. C-C♯, or E-F)
	interval	The distance between two musical tones, keys on the keyboard, or notes on the staff. (Ex. 2nd, 3rd, 4th, 5th)
	key signature	The key signature appears at the beginning of each line of music. It indicates sharps or flats to be used throughout the piece.
	ledger line	A short line used to extend the staff.
	legato	Smooth, connected.
	major scale	An eight-note scale with half steps between scale degrees 3-4 and 7-8.
	natural	A natural (always a white key) cancels a sharp or a flat.
	octave	The interval which spans 8 letter names. (Ex. C to C)
	ottava	Play one octave higher (or lower) than written.
	pedal change	Shows the down-up motion of the damper pedal.
	phrase	A musical sentence. A phrase is often shown by a slur, also called a phrase mark.
	primary chords	The I, IV, and V chords are the primary chords in any major key.
	quarter note	One count or beat. (One-quarter the value of a whole note.)
	quarter rest	One beat of silence.
	repeat sign	Play the music within the repeat signs again.
	ritardando	Gradually slowing down.
	root position	The letter name of the chord is the lowest note.
	scale	From the Latin word *scala*, meaning "ladder." The notes of a scale move up or down by 2nds (steps).
	second (2nd) (step)	The interval that spans two letter names. (Ex. C up to D, or F down to E) On the staff: line-to-the-next-space or space-to-the-next-line.
	sharp	A sharp raises the note one half step.
	sixth (6th)	The interval that spans six letter names. (Ex. E up to C, or D down to F) On the staff a 6th is written line-(skip 2 lines)-space or space-(skip 2 spaces)-line.
	slur	A curved line that indicates legato playing.
	staccato	Detached, disconnected.
	tempo	The speed of the music.
	third (3rd) (skip)	The interval that spans three letter names. (Ex. C up to E, or F down to D) On the staff: line-to-the-next-line or space-to-the-next-space.
	tie	A curved line that connects two notes on the same line or space. Hold for the total counts of both notes.
	time signature	Two numbers at the beginning of a piece (one above the other). The top number indicates the number of beats per measure; the bottom number represents the note receiving the beat.
	triad	A 3-note chord built in 3rds.
	upbeat (pick-up note)	The note(s) of an incomplete opening measure.
	whole note	Four counts or beats.
	whole rest	Silence for any whole measure. (Hangs below line 4)
	whole step	The distance of two half steps.

ALPHABETICAL INDEX OF TITLES